THIS BOOK BELONGS TO:

_____

COLORING PAGES

THANKSGIVING THINGS

HOW TO DRAW

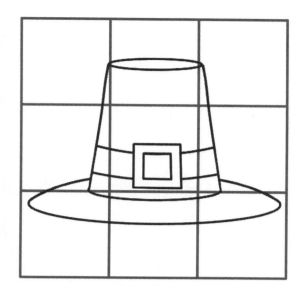

Trace & Draw

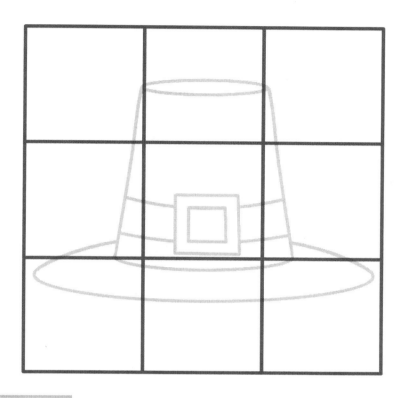

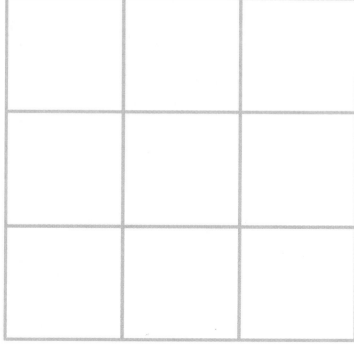

Trace & Draw

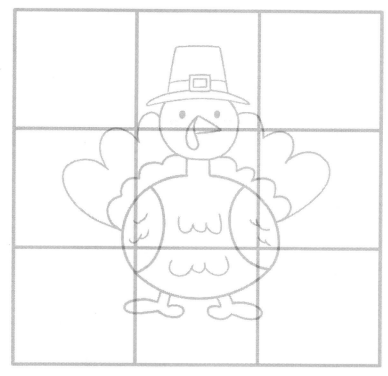

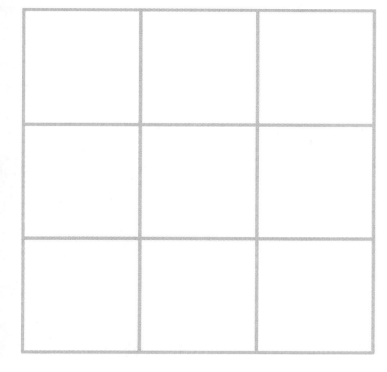

Trace & Draw

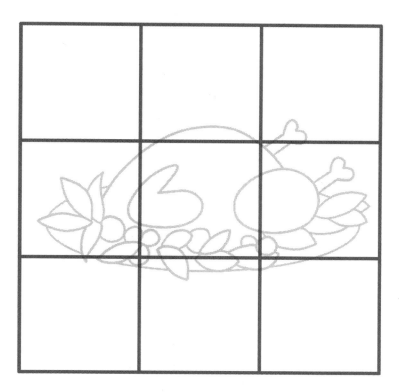

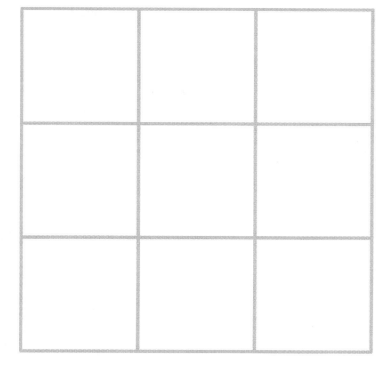

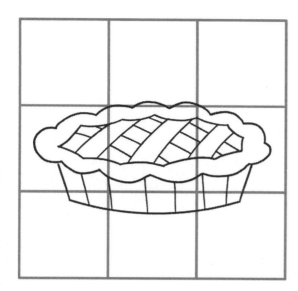

Trace & Draw

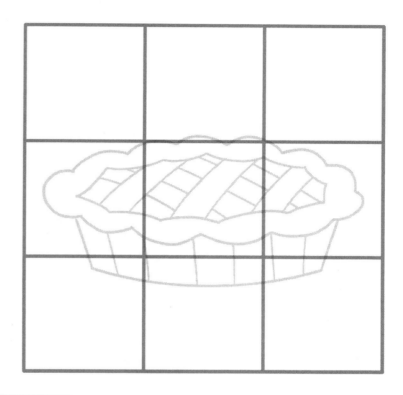

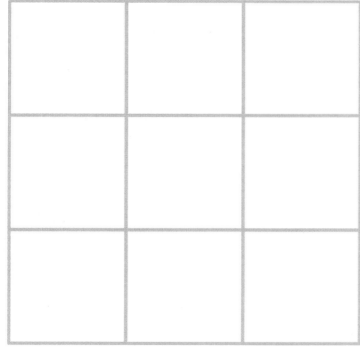

MATH PUZZLES

LILA AND SOFI'S AUTUMN LEAF BUSINESS

Lila and Sofi are best friends who started a leaf-raking business this fall. They work together to help their neighbors clean up autumn leaves. Here's how their business works:

- They charge $5 for each bag of leaves they fill.
- Lila and Sofi share the money equally.
- Together, they can fill 3 bags in one hour.

Last weekend, they worked for 2 hours on Saturday and 3 hours on Sunday.

Questions:

1. How many bags did they fill on Saturday?
2. How many bags did they fill on Sunday?
3. How many bags did they fill in total over the weekend?
4. How much money did they earn in total?
5. If they share the money equally, how much did each girl get?

LILA AND SOFI'S AUTUMN LEAF BUSINESS

Use the space below to take notes and calculate your answers.

THANKSGIVING DINNER MATHS

Mashed Potato Mountain

Jack is mashing potatoes. He mashes 4 potatoes, then 3 more, and finally 2 more. How many potatoes did he mash in total?

Cranberry Counting

Sally is making cranberry sauce. The recipe calls for 25 cranberries, but she accidentally added 5 extra. How many cranberries did she use?

Thanksgiving Dinner Time

Thanksgiving dinner is at 5:00 PM. It's now 2:30 PM. How many hours and minutes are left until dinner time?

THANKSGIVING DINNER MATHS

Leftover Turkey Sandwiches

After Thanksgiving, the Johnson family has enough leftover turkey to make 15 sandwiches. If each person eats 3 sandwiches, how many people can have sandwiches?

Enough Pumpkin Pie for Everyone?

Grandma Jo bakes 2 pumpkin pies. Each pie is divided into 6 slices. There are 10 people sitting at the dinner table. How many slices of pie are there in total? Is there enough pie for everyone?

CHALLENGING THANKSGIVING MATHS

The Pilgrims' Journey

The Pilgrims traveled for 66 days to reach America. They left England on September 16th. What date did they arrive?

Use the calendars below to count the days!

SEPTEMBER 1620

Sun	Mon	Tue	Wed	Thu	Fri	Sat
		1	2	3	4	5
6	7	8	9	10	11	12
13	14	15	16	17	18	19
20	21	22	23	24	25	26
27	28	29	30			

OCTOBER 1620

Sun	Mon	Tue	Wed	Thu	Fri	Sat
				1	2	3
4	5	6	7	8	9	10
11	12	13	14	15	16	17
18	19	20	21	22	23	24
25	26	27	28	29	30	31

NOVEMBER 1620

Sun	Mon	Tue	Wed	Thu	Fri	Sat
1	2	3	4	5	6	7
8	9	10	11	12	13	14
15	16	17	18	19	20	21
22	23	24	25	26	27	28
29	30					

Thanksgiving Shopping

Mom is buying ingredients for Thanksgiving dinner. She needs 3 cans of cranberry sauce at $2 each, 2 boxes of stuffing mix at $3 each, and a turkey that costs $20. How much money will she spend in total?

CHALLENGING THANKSGIVING MATHS

Tom the Turkey

Tom the Turkey has 15 tail feathers. 5 are red, 4 are yellow, and the rest are blue. How many blue feathers does Tom have?

Parade Balloons

In the Thanksgiving parade, there are balloons shaped like:

- 5 turkeys
- 3 pumpkin pies
- 4 autumn leaves

Each balloon needs 2 people to hold it.

Questions: a) How many balloons are there in total? b) How many people are needed to hold all the balloons?

THANKSGIVING MATH SOLUTIONS

Mashed Potato Mountain
Solution: 4 + 3 + 2 = 9 potatoes
Cranberry Counting
Solution: 25 + 5 = 30 cranberries
Thanksgiving Dinner Time
Solution: 2 hours and 30 minutes

Leftover Turkey Sandwiches
Solution: 15 ÷ 3 = 5 people
Enough Pumpkin Pie for Everyone?
Solution: 2 x 6 = 12 slices total.

Challenging Thanksgiving Maths

The Pilgrims' Journey
Answer: The Pilgrims arrived on November 21, 1620.

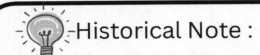 Historical Note :

A long time ago, people used a different calendar called the **Julian Calendar**, which is why some old historical documents say the Pilgrims landed at Plymouth on November 11.

According to the calendar we use today, called the **Gregorian Calendar**, that date is actually November 21.

Calendar Explanations:
- **Julian Calendar**: This was the old way of counting days, created by Julius Caesar. It wasn't perfect and made the year a little too long.
- **Gregorian Calendar**: This is the calendar we use today. It was created by Pope Gregory XIII to fix the old calendar, and it helps keep our dates and seasons in better order.

The Pilgrims' Journey
Solution: The Pilgrims arrived on November 21, 1620.
Thanksgiving Shopping
Solution: (3 × $2) + (2 × $3) + $20 = $6 + $6 + $20 = $32
Tom the Turkey
Solution: 15 - 5 - 4 = 6 blue feathers
Parade Balloons
Answers: a) 5 + 3 + 4 = 12 balloons in total b) 12 balloons × 2 people per balloon = 24 people needed

THANKSGIVING MATH SOLUTIONS

Lila and Sofi's Autumn Leaf Business

Number of bags filled:
Saturday: 2 hours × 3 bags per hour = 6 bags
Sunday: 3 hours × 3 bags per hour = 9 bags
Total bags: 6 + 9 = **15 bags**

Total money earned:
15 bags × $5 per bag = **$75**

Money each girl received:
Total money ÷ 2 = $75 ÷ 2 = **$37.50 each**

READING & COMPREHENSION & WORD GAMES

THE STORY OF THE FIRST THANKSGIVING

Once upon a time, way back in the year 1620, a group of people called the Pilgrims decided they no longer wanted to live in England. They wanted to practice their religion freely, without anyone telling them how to do it. So, they hopped aboard a creaky old ship named the Mayflower, which was about as comfortable as a lumpy mattress filled with porcupines.

After a long, tough journey across the big blue ocean that lasted 66 days, the Pilgrims spotted land. But they were in for a surprise! They had originally meant to land near what is now New York City, but instead, they found themselves in a place called Plymouth (what is now Massachusetts).

The Pilgrims weren't the first people here, though. Native Americans, including the Wampanoag tribe, had been living on this land for thousands of years. The Native Americans were experts at fishing, hunting, and growing yummy vegetables like corn.

That first winter was really hard for the Pilgrims. Many got sick, and they didn't have enough food. But then something amazing happened. Two Native Americans, named Samoset and Squanto, came to help. Squanto spoke English and taught the Pilgrims how to plant corn, catch fish, and survive in their new home.

The Pilgrims and the Wampanoag made a peace agreement. They promised to help protect each other.

When spring came, the Pilgrims planted crops, and by fall, they had their first good harvest. They were so happy that they decided to have a big celebration.

The Pilgrims started their party by shooting their guns in the air. This made the Wampanoag worry that there might be trouble. Their leader, Massasoit, came to check things out with 90 of his men. But when they arrived, they saw it was just a harvest celebration. The Wampanoag decided to join in, and they even brought deer to add to the feast.

For three whole days, the Pilgrims and Wampanoag ate together, played games, and had fun. They enjoyed foods like deer, corn, fish, and roasted meat. This celebration became known as the First Thanksgiving.

It's important to remember that while this was a happy time, things didn't stay peaceful forever.

In the years that followed, there were many conflicts between the settlers and the Native Americans. Today, Thanksgiving means different things to different people. For some, it's a time to be thankful, while for others, especially many Native Americans, it's a day to remember their history and culture.

Today, when we celebrate Thanksgiving, we remember this story of two different groups of people coming together to share a meal and give thanks for what they had.

✏️Critical Thinking Time

In the story, the Pilgrims were grateful when the Wampanoag helped them. Can you think of a time when someone helped you and how it made you feel? Have you ever helped someone who was thankful?

_____

_____

_____

_____

_____

_____

_____

_____

_____

_____

_____

Thankfulness Jar

Write down all the big and small things you are grateful for. Take your time, and feel free to come back to this page anytime to add more as you remember.

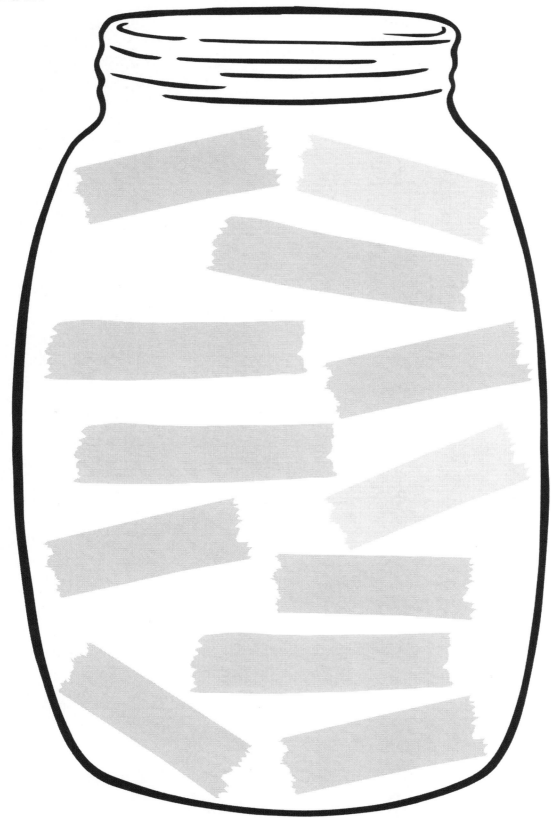

WORD SEARCH

Countries where Thanksgiving is a holiday

```
              Y G U
              Y R P
              I Q V
          E K S D I
          V T A E T
          B R N C Q
        I Q Q D T P A N D
        N V H R A C V N C P
    W V W R Z K X L K D H A V K M
    S W R X P M D U U X H E D Y R
  K T Q F O I N C W M C Y X N X T A Z C K U
Y W H X B A P G G Y B I B H V Z Y K J J J I
G G B J D H S D F W A T B W E N Z R M T L
I I C V A I R H U N I T E D S T A T E S
N O S N L I L Y K W C Y C Y I U H L
    U E R P U D V A H N V H P C
    R E O I L I B E R I A A K
    G Z C R R H B A M J Z X A
    V L T S B L M U S M G Z
    S S L G U N E Z Z U R
    A Q X D P T M W S
        F Z C A O
      F           C
      X         J G K L
```

UNITED STATES
SANTA LUCIA
GRENADA
LIBERIA
CANADA

Countries that celebrate harvest festivals!
(but not Thanksgiving)

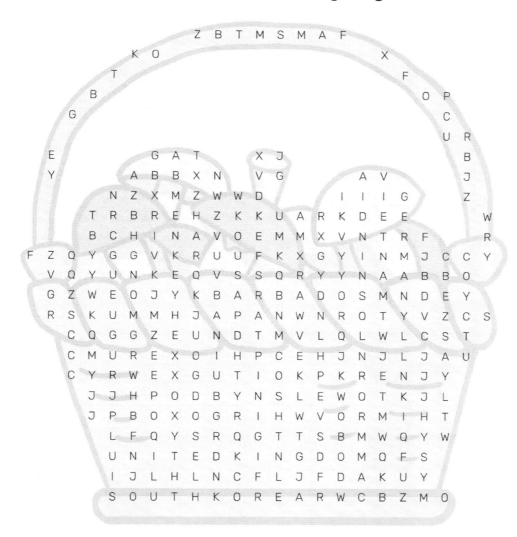

```
              Z B T M S M A F
          K O                   X
        T                         F
      B                         O   P
    G                           C     R
                                U       R
  E       G A T     X J                 B
  Y     A B B X N   V G       A V       J
      N Z X M Z W W D     I I I G     Z
    T R B R E H Z K K U A R K D E E
    B C H I N A V O E M M X V N T R F   R
F Z Q Y G G V K R U U F K X G Y I N M J C C Y
V Q Y U N K E Q V S S Q R Y Y N A A B B O
G Z W E O J Y K B A R B A D O S M N D E Y
R S K U M M H J A P A N W N R O T Y V Z C S
C Q G G Z E U N D T M V L Q L W L C S T
C M U R E X O I H P C E H J N J L J A U
C Y R W E X G U T I O K P K R E N J Y
  J J H P O D B Y N S L E W O T K J L
  J P B O X O G R I H W V O R M I H T
    L F Q Y S R Q G T T S B M W Q Y W
    U N I T E D K I N G D O M Q F S
    I J L H L N C F L J F D A K U Y
      S O U T H K O R E A R W C B Z M O
```

Search for the country name, not the name of the holiday that is in parenthesis.

South Korea (Chuseok)

India (Pongal)

Barbados (Crop Over)   Vietnam (Tết Trung Thu)

Germany (Erntedankfest)   China (Mid-Autumn Festival)

Japan (Niinamesai)   United Kingdom (Harvest Festival)

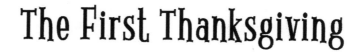

WORD SEARCH

The First Thanksgiving

```
M Z P A S P W Y C
R E L T F E A S T K
G C Y K T W V F U Q
R A M X N Z W P P F
A E O S Q U A N T O
T P U W P D S I J V
I Q T M Z I O H C V
T A H T A W L S D L
E U P U Z R Y L G V X
P D T O E F S F H R V V
S E O S Z M L S L G I G
T S A M O S E T M O R M
Z W O Q R W F P D U A C U W N S J X
A A M J J O W A M P A N O A G J B E E Y T S G
H A R V E S T Z O J E G Q N M Q Y Y R W K R J
N A T I V E A M E R I C A N S D
```

FEAST
HARVEST
NATIVE AMERICANS
PILGRIMS
SAMOSET
WAMPANOAG

GRATITUDE
MAYFLOWER
PEACE
PLYMOUTH
SQUANTO

Thanksgiving Dinner

```
              N W S                    S
          F E H H F E R F          G T
          E E T O C R O M M B D P
      M U Y U P P Y N T A Y H I
    W S K Q N D L D G A C D T N D              Q L
      U S O H M A H Y Y T A E D N D S W Z      B
  X G   F D Y J R Z U P E M R F O N X O E T H X W U
    Y Q C R B W C F V R R W W E P D Q I R G U N U F N W S O
  A S A M G H E W M R J B Q H S D C M K R F T R R J E P P K
  J I J I S Y S T U F F I N G A W E H K Q O Y F K K K N R W R
  V E J O B V A R C M G T R A M R H E L E L M A W M E N K P
  H S N W A J R D F M B O Q K B S E L J L Q R M J M Y J V
      D C R P P A U R Y C L B R A S F A S J N L S Z X
        G Y V E L A K I M L I M E S T G V M E
          E
```

CORNBREAD
HAM
STUFFING

DINNER ROLLS
MAC AND CHEESE
TURKEY

GRAVY
MASHED POTATOES
YAMS

Which is your favorite Pie Flavor?

```
              R J              F
          A S J S M B C T H R F W U X
        U I Z Z P T H B W D I R H A X R C X U
      J K C R T V P D X O U E N I A P R A R E S C V
    S F W H V U E L C M G O T E R W N I H K P Q I W S
    C A X E J Z I E L J L V F T T Y S B H S T E R L B
    T Q R S N I A G U S D M D L E P M B E O T O G X Y
    L S M G U J D Z K L K K Y R O F M R W L B
    O J T Q W N Y Z T U W J Y M T A X R O G
    P U M P K I N N K M E Q G H I A C G Y F
    M J V J I I W V F F L W K N L L T R U
      Z O D D U F G F W I K K N L K O
              I B P E C A N P
```

APPLE   BUTTERMILK
CHESS   CRANBERRY
PECAN   PUMPKIN
SHOOFLY   SWEET POTATO

Countries where Thanksgiving is a holiday

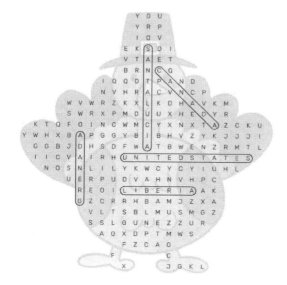

Countries that celebrate harvest festivals!
(but not Thanksgiving)

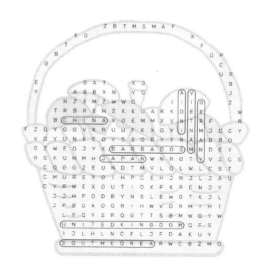

The First Thanksgiving

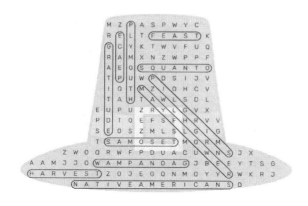

Thanksgiving Dinner

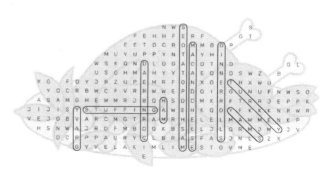

Which is your favorite Pie Flavor?

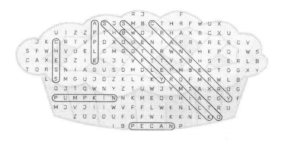

Thanksgiving Would You Rather

How to Play

Number of player: 2 or more

Instructions:

#1 Pick a Judge. For every round players will take turns being the judge.

If you can't decide on who goes first : Let's go in alphabetical order! The person who's name begins with a letter closest to the letter A begins the game and so on.

#2 Pick a Question.

The next five pages of this book have fun "Would You Rather" questions. The judge will pick any of these question and ask it out loud. Each player will take picking one of the "would you rather" choices and explaining why they made their pick.

#3 The Best Answer is...

The judge then decides who came up with the best answer.

The best answer can be either the most creative answer or the funniest.

Here is an example:

Question:

Would you rather have a pet
Sea monster
or a
Giant bat

Pete's answer: A sea monster because she can take my whole family a free cruise trip.

Thomas' answer: A giant bat because he can fly me to school when I wake up late and miss the bus.

Judge's decision: Thomas because it would be awesome to sleep in and not worry about being late for school.

WOULD YOU RATHER
EAT TURKEY-FLAVORED ICE CREAM
OR
DRINK GRAVY-FLAVORED MILKSHAKES?

WOULD YOU RATHER
HAVE A PET TURKEY THAT CAN TALK
OR
HAVE A PUMPKIN THAT CAN SING?

WOULD YOU RATHER
BE ABLE TO TURN ANYTHING YOU TOUCH INTO MASHED POTATOES
OR
BE ABLE TO MAKE CRANBERRY SAUCE RAIN FROM THE SKY?

WOULD YOU RATHER

EAT YOUR THANKSGIVING DINNER WHILE WEARING MITTENS

OR

EAT YOUR ENTIRE MEAL USING CHOPSTICKS?

WOULD YOU RATHER

WEAR A TURKEY COSTUME TO SCHOOL FOR ONE DAY

OR

GOBBLE LIKE A TURKEY EVERY TIME SOMEONE SAYS YOUR NAME FOR A WEEK?

WOULD YOU RATHER

HAVE A THANKSGIVING FEAST FOR BREAKFAST EVERY DAY

OR

HAVE A PLATTER OF THANKSGIVING DESSERTS FOR DINNER EVERY NIGHT?

WOULD YOU RATHER

HAVE HAIR THAT CHANGES COLOR LIKE FALL LEAVES

OR

HAVE CLOTHES THAT ALWAYS SMELL LIKE FRESH-BAKED PUMPKIN PIE?

WOULD YOU RATHER

TEACH TURKEYS HOW TO DANCE

OR

TEACH SQUIRRELS HOW TO BAKE PIES?

WOULD YOU RATHER

RIDE TO SCHOOL ON A GIANT TURKEY

OR

SAIL TO SCHOOL IN A BOAT MADE FROM A HOLLOWED-OUT PUMPKIN?

THANKSGIVING JOKES

What kind of music did the Pilgrims listen to?
Plymouth Rock!

What do you call a running turkey?
Fast food!

What do you call a turkey on the day after Thanksgiving?
Lucky!

Why did the cranberries turn red?
They saw the turkey dressing!

What key has legs and can't open doors?
A tur-key!

Knock knock!
Who's there?
Arthur.
Arthur who?
Arthur any leftovers?

Knock knock!
Who's there?
Dewey.
Dewey who?
Dewey have to wait long for dinner?

Knock knock!
Who's there?
Norma Lee.
Norma Lee who?
Norma Lee I don't eat this much!

Knock knock!
Who's there?
Dishes.
Dishes who?
Dishes the best Thanksgiving ever!

The Funniest Thanksgiving Fill-in-the-Blank Stories

How to Play:

1. Don't read the stories yet! Cover the story part of the page with a piece of paper.
2. Fill in each blank with the type of word asked for.
3. After filling in all the blanks, uncover the story and read the stories out loud.
4. Laugh at your silly Thanksgiving stories!

When filling in the blanks, remember:

- Noun: A person, place, or thing (like "turkey" or "kitchen")
- Verb: An action word (like "dance" or "gobble")
- Adjective: A word that describes (like "fluffy" or "smelly")

The Silly Turkey Day Tale

On Thanksgiving Day, our (**1. Adjective**) family gathered around the table. The room was filled with delicious smells and happy (**2. Noun (plural)**). Mom was busy (**3. Verb ending in -ing**) in the kitchen, while Dad set the table with our best (**4. Noun**).

Suddenly, we heard a (**5. Adjective**) noise coming from outside. We looked out the window and saw a giant (**6. Noun (food)**) (**7. Verb**) down the street! Everyone started to (**8. Verb**), but then we realized it was just Uncle Bob in his silly (**9. Noun (animal)**) costume.

We all laughed and sat down to (**10. Verb**) our delicious Thanksgiving feast. It was the funniest Thanksgiving ever!

1. Adjective: _____

2. Noun (plural): _____

3. Verb (ending in -ing): _____

4. Noun: _____

5. Adjective: _____

6. Noun (food): _____

7. Verb: _____

8. Verb: _____

9. Noun (animal): _____

10. Verb: _____

The Great Thanksgiving Pie Mystery

Grandma's (**1. Adjective**) pie disappeared from the kitchen (**2. Noun**) on Thanksgiving morning. The family (**3. Verb, past tense**) around, sniffing for clues like hungry dogs. All that was left was a trail of (**4. Adjective**) crumbs leading to the (**5. Noun**).

As they (**6. Verb, past tense**), a (**7. Adjective**) sound came from behind the (**8. Noun**). Aunt Betty (**9. Verb, past tense**) the cupboard. There sat Fluffy the cat, her (**10. Adjective**) face covered in pie filling, looking very pleased with herself.

The family burst out laughing at the sight. Grandma decided to (**11. Verb**) another pie. Meanwhile, Fluffy licked her paws, already planning her next tasty trick.

From that day on, pies at Grandma's house needed extra security!

1. _____ (Adjective)

2. _____ (Noun)

3. _____ (Verb, past tense)

4. _____ (Adjective)

5. _____ (Noun)

6. _____ (Verb, past tense)

7. _____ (Adjective)

8. _____ (Noun)

9. _____ (Verb, past tense)

10. _____ (Adjective)

11. _____ (Verb)

SUDOKU

SUDOKU

Puzzle #1

2				7		8	4	6
1	6	7			8		9	2
		9	3	2		1	5	7
6	8	5	9		4	7	2	
	7		2			4		9
4	9	2		1	7	5	8	3
7		6	8		2			4
5	2			9	1	6	3	
9		8		6		2		

Puzzle #2

	7	9	5	1	2		8	
	1				9	2		3
4	2	8	6	7	3	5		1
6	9		1	3	5	7	4	
		8	2	6	9	1	5
1	8			9	4	3		2
9	4	3				8		7
2	6		9	5	8	1		4
		1				6		

Puzzle #3

		8	4		9			
1	5	9	2	3	7	6	4	8
2		6	5	1	8	3	7	9
		1			2	4	9	7
		5		4		2		
		4		8	1		3	6
	1	7		2		9	5	3
5	9				4	8	6	2
8	6	2		9		7	1	

SUDOKU

Puzzle #4

							4	2
	1	9			4	5	8	
2	4	3	5	7	8		9	
	9			2		8	5	
8		2	4		5	9	1	
1	5	6	7	8	9	2		4
	8		6	1	2			
9	2	7	8	4		1		5
6	3	1	9	5	7		2	8

SUDOKU

Puzzle #1

2	5	3	1	7	9	8	4	6
1	6	7	5	4	8	3	9	2
8	4	9	3	2	6	1	5	7
6	8	5	9	3	4	7	2	1
3	7	1	2	8	5	4	6	9
4	9	2	6	1	7	5	8	3
7	3	6	8	5	2	9	1	4
5	2	4	7	9	1	6	3	8
9	1	8	4	6	3	2	7	5

Puzzle #2

3	7	9	5	1	2	4	8	6
5	1	6	4	8	9	2	7	3
4	2	8	6	7	3	5	9	1
6	9	2	1	3	5	7	4	8
7	3	4	8	2	6	9	1	5
1	8	5	7	9	4	3	6	2
9	4	3	2	6	1	8	5	7
2	6	7	9	5	8	1	3	4
8	5	1	3	4	7	6	2	9

Puzzle #3

7	3	8	4	6	9	1	2	5
1	5	9	2	3	7	6	4	8
2	4	6	5	1	8	3	7	9
3	8	1	6	5	2	4	9	7
6	7	5	9	4	3	2	8	1
9	2	4	7	8	1	5	3	6
4	1	7	8	2	6	9	5	3
5	9	3	1	7	4	8	6	2
8	6	2	3	9	5	7	1	4

Puzzle #4

5	6	8	3	9	1	7	4	2
7	1	9	2	6	4	5	8	3
2	4	3	5	7	8	6	9	1
3	9	4	1	2	6	8	5	7
8	7	2	4	3	5	9	1	6
1	5	6	7	8	9	2	3	4
4	8	5	6	1	2	3	7	9
9	2	7	8	4	3	1	6	5
6	3	1	9	5	7	4	2	8

MAZES

MAZE #6

Made in the USA
Columbia, SC
18 November 2024

46951795R00059